CLASSIC MARQUES

Duple Coachbuilders
From Domination to Demise

CHRISTOPHER G SIMS

NOSTALGIA ROAD

First published by Crécy Publishing Ltd 2013

A CIP record for this book is available from
the British Library

ISBN 9781908 347121

Printed in Malta by Melita Press

Nostalgia Road is an imprint of
Crécy Publishing Limited
1a Ringway Trading Estate
Shadowmoss Road
Manchester M22 5LH

www.crecy.co.uk

Front Cover: Without doubt the best looking Duple Vega/Super Vega produced, this version was introduced in 1954. By this time the SB chassis had grown and the body was designed to accommodate 41 passengers. Engine choices were the traditional petrol or the newer diesel (heavy oil). The swoops along the coach's body and its 'butterfly' grille hit the mark!

Rear Cover Top: This was one of the first Duple-bodied Bedfords, dating to 1935. The chassis was a Bedford WTB and the vehicle could accommodate 26 passengers.

Rear Cover Bottom: Pictured arriving at the East Anglian Transport Museum, Carlton Colville, this was the final Dominant bus body built and was fitted to a Leyland TRCTL11/2RZ. It had a wide, four-leaf, entrance door and seating for 62 in a high-floor saloon.

Contents Page: These two coaches illustrate the changes to the rear end of the Super Vega of the period between 1959 and 1962, on the left, with that of the Vega from the mid-1950s.

All illustrations are from the author's collection or have been supplied by David Gladwin except as indicated.

Acknowledgements

In completing this book, there are a number of people I must thank for their help. Firstly, Peter Waller and Crécy Publishing, who both showed faith in a novice writer and gave me the opportunity to chronicle Duple's story. My good friend David Gladwin — he of many transport titles and magazine articles — proved invaluable to my task through his knowledge on completing books and knack for unearthing terrific period and official Duple pictures. I'd also like to thank G R Mills and K A Fuller, who gave kind permission for the use of their images. Finally, I'd like to thank my wife Cindy, who guided me through sending e-mails and typed up my text — a great help, support and secretary. And finally to you, the reader; I sincerely hope you enjoy my first published title — after a few prototypes, you have the finished model!

Christopher G Sims, 2013

CONTENTS

Introduction

The complete history of Duple coach-building has been well documented by respected transport writers in the past. It would, therefore, be a fruitless and uninteresting exercise to assemble facts and figures that have been in print many times. With that in mind, I would like to focus on Duple's fortunes from 1950, when the company was unquestionably the busiest and most in demand coachbody supplier in the land.

Our journey will end nearly 40 years later in 1989, when after trying to fight the spread of the foreign-built coach body and witnessing both of the UK's main lightweight chassis suppliers throwing in the towel, stark financial realities of dwindling sales and the more demanding customer, saw Duple have its final models produced and sold by main rival, Plaxton.

As your author has no intention of sounding vague, a few paragraphs explaining Duple's origins would seem a sensible way to feed into the story.

This brand-new Duple 340, fitted on a Leyland chassis, was supplied as one of a batch of five coaches to Highland Scottish — Nos E271-E275 — in April 1987. The plastic sheets over the passenger seats indicate that the vehicle had yet to enter service. The rear continental exit, tinted glazing and fitted curtains provided a luxurious atmosphere for long-distance travel.

Registered in February 1948, this Duple Vista 29-seat body was fitted to a Bedford OB chassis and supplied to Kendricks Transport Ltd Dudley in Worcestershire.

In early 1959 Vauxhall sent this Duple Super Vega-bodied Bedford and other vehicles on a six-month sales tour of Europe. The coach was painted white and poppy red and carried a suitable slogan on the side.

Duple's Origins

Duple Bodies & Motors Ltd was established in December 1919 by Herbert R White. He had served as an apprentice ironmonger and had also been a dairy farmer. His first premises for coach-building were in Hornsey, London, and, to allow expansion, new premises were acquired in Hendon, Middlesex, during 1925. From then on, Duple established itself as a major player in, firstly, the motor charabanc sector, bodying double- and single-deck buses by 1930, and then, in 1932/33, introduced the true motor-coach with new levels of comport and durability — standards to which all body suppliers strived for in terms of elegance, strength and luxury.

Duple forged a reputation for quality and style that graced many chassis types. This activity progressed steadily until the hostilities of World War 2 hit the country, during which all efforts from bodybuilding concerns were redirected into almost everything needed for the war effort. The government had the decisions on what was built.

Restricted body construction carried on during the war years, with all vehicles supplied being Spartan outside and in, being devoid of trim and extravagance. Single- or double-deck, these were known as 'utility' bodies. Duple did not regain normal patterns of workload and output until the 1940s had passed.

A 32-seat Duple Mark II body fitted to a Bedford chassis was described in the original caption from late 1943 as 'virtually a de luxe edition of the original Utility bus.' The total cost, including chassis and leather seats, was £1,010.

Right: An advert that was featured on a front cover of *Passenger Transport* from January 1950 shows a typical single-deck product from the company fitted to an AEC chassis.

Opposite page: This was one of the first Duple-bodied Bedfords, dating to 1935. The chassis was a Bedford WTB and the vehicle could accommodate 26 passengers.

JERSEY AIRPORTS

COACHWORK
by

COACHBUILDERS   TO THE WORLD

DUPLE MOTOR BODIES, LTD., THE HYDE, HENDON, LONDON, N.W.9.

Duple in the 1950s

Optimism in the industry was back by 1950, the shackles and problems of the war years were fading and Duple was producing designs with promise again. This would be the decade that Duple Ltd would become the coach industries' major supplier.

The company was building bodies in 1950 that are regarded as true classics today. Heavyweight chassis from AEC, Daimler, Leyland and Maudslay carried the stylish, half-cab A-type body. Its curved waist-rail and window line, coupled with sumptuous interiors of quality materials and polished fittings, seduced the fussiest of passengers.

The B-type body was a less curvaceous product; it had straight side window pillars, but still the curved side flashes. Again destined for heavyweight chassis, but lacking the luxury of the A-type, this was really an early forerunner of the dual-purpose coach. Duple was also producing bodies for underfloor chassis in 1950 that would soon render the half-cab coach body obsolete. The Roadmaster was built exclusively for the Leyland Royal Tiger and was a handsome vehicle that featured a front entrance ahead of the steering axle. The body had shallow windows that could be fixed bays or fitted with sliding ventilation; its windscreen, entrance and first short window bay were deeper with straight trim at floor level.

DUPLE PROUDLY PRESENT...

The 'Vega'!

THE striking, progressive design of this eagerly-awaited coach amply fulfils all expectations. Built for the new Bedford chassis—available either as luxury coach or service bus—it has the new, fully-enclosed front that allows perfect, all-round visibility for driver and passengers. In every detail the Duple-Bedford "Vega" represents a great step forward in coachbuilding!

We are pleased to announce that our Repair and Service Department is now re-opened for repairs and renovations to all coachwork.

Duple-Bedford "Vega" metal-framed coach, mounted only on Bedford chassis. 33 seats. Ample baggage-room. Also available as service bus. Coach complete £2,190 including chassis. Mark VI complete £1,960 including chassis.

Coachbuilders to the world

DUPLE MOTOR BODIES LTD., THE HYDE, HENDON, LONDON, N.W.9.

Featured in the advert on a front cover of *Passenger Transport* from January 1950 was the new Vega body as fitted to a Bedford. The price of the complete coach, fitted with 33 seats, was £2,190.

Opposite page: Belonging to Felix, Long Melford, Suffolk, this 29-seat Bedford OB was built around 1950. This type are the most popular of all the preserved Bedford/Duple combinations. Many survive and are much admired and cherished.

Bought brand new in 1953 by the Carter family of Litcham, near Swaffham in Norfolk, this unusual body style was named the Coronation. The basic Vega style was reworked with slightly different side trim, much deeper windscreens and a very ornate front grille design. When photographed here the coach was 11 years old. *G R Mills*

Another design for underfloor chassis buyers was the Duple Ambassador, which was built on products from AEC, Dennis and Guy. Its construction was more in keeping with 1950 as this featured the more traditional centre entrance and the curved trim and window-line from coaches of the previous era. Although having a full-width front it was clearly not as modern as its Roadmaster stable-mate. This was not helped by a heavy curve under the windscreen that raised to the centre and drooped at the edges, the corner pillars were inset and the glazing from the sides curved around the front to meet these. A later restyle gave the Ambassador a deeper windscreen and first window bay, the waist and window line were noticeably straighter and the whole effect looked heavy and cumbersome, lacking the style and flair of the half-cab bodies that had gone before.

The Bedford OB — the most popular lightweight coach of its time — carried more Duple bodies than any other builder. Today, in 2012, a sizeable number of these survive and are much cherished for their nostalgic feel, their presence at events and use in operation for special private hires. If a thatched cottage with a garden full of flowers is most peoples' idyll of a 'chocolate box home', surely then a Duple Vista-bodied Bedford OB is the PSV equivalent.

Dating from the early 1950s, this is a Duple Elizabethan heavyweight centre-entrance coach. It is recorded in the livery of Cronshaw, of London, an operator that had an operating base in Lancashire to serve Blackpool and the many who worked in the county's factories and mills. The chassis was a Leyland Tiger Cub. *David Gladwin*

Not resting on its laurels, Vauxhall Motors was developing a larger capacity replacement in the background and, in September 1950, three prototype Bedford SB chassis were dispatched to Duple for bodying. These pioneers started the most numerically popular body-builder/chassis combination in coach history, a relationship that continued for over 35 years.

The SB featured forward-control steering that dispensed with the front wings, exposed headlamps, engine bonnet and radiator cowl. The running gear and lights would, from now on, be encapsulated within the bodywork, allowing Duple to style from the very front to the back.

The original Vega body, bulbous in appearance with the capacity to accommodate 33 passengers, was often known and marketed as the Big Bedford. This early body went largely unchanged until 1953, when, for one season, Duple built the Coronation body.

The basic Vega gained restyled side mouldings and a very ornate front-end that made the Coronation appear less curvy and friendly than the Vega. The new body looked more purposeful and modern, and coincided with Princess Elizabeth's accession to the throne. Unlike the OB Vista, very few of these survive today and, if there are half-a-dozen left in the country, I would be surprised.

During 1952, Duple bought the business of Nudd Brothers & Lockyer Ltd, which built coaches at Kegworth, Leicestershire. It had spent many years making all-metal bodies and Duple quickly renamed the operation Duple Motor Bodies (Midland).

Taken on a sunny day at Litcham in 1961, this was the original Duple Vega built on the 31ft Bedford SB chassis. Despite its age, the vehicle was still in an immaculate condition with not a dent to be seen. *G R Mills*

This is an original Duple Vega, which increased capacity by four seats and was fitted to the Bedford SB chassis. Very bulbous in appearance, the Vega was an instant success and dominated coach sales in the 1950s.

Without doubt the best looking Duple Vega/Super Vega produced, this version was introduced in 1954. By this time the SB chassis had grown and the body was designed to accommodate 41 passengers. Engine choices were the traditional petrol or the newer diesel (heavy oil). The swoops along the coach's body and its 'butterfly' grille hit the mark!

The lightweight Vega was a roaring sales success and, in 1953, a freshly styled body replaced the bulbous, curvy original. Despite the cove panels being nicely rounded, the body sides were virtually flat though gently curving around the front and rear. The waist-rail was subtly sloped and a deeper screen and first window bay were used. A simple, rather dull oval shaped grille shielded the front radiator.

This revamp was very short-lived and the new classic 'butterfly front' Super Vega was announced in 1954. The body featured a new rear window arrangement that comprised a shallow, high set rear pane flanked by almost triangular curved corner bays. The illuminated name board sat between these and below the rear window. The rear-most side pillars raked gently backwards to meet up with the corner glazing. The whole effect gave a light, airy feel inside the coach and, from the outside, side trim options of simple curves or dramatic swoops and dips made this style of body without doubt the prettiest Duple offering on an SB chassis. This style would reign virtually unaltered until 1959.

A new body, named Britannia, was introduced in 1955; this was to be built on heavyweight chassis from AEC and Leyland and featured a centre-entrance, still commonplace in the mid-1950s. It borrowed some design traits from its Super Vega stable-mate. The sloped waist-rail and three-piece rear window arrangement suited the larger body well, with side trim options to suit the buyers' preferences. A circular roundel could be specified in the design, as with the Super Vega, to incorporate a company's badge or logo.

The Alpine body made its first appearance in 1957. In its original form this was a Super Vega body not only with front and rear Perspex roof panels, but toughened glass quarter-lights to both sides of the cove panels also. This was intended to give improved vision where trips and tours included tall landmarks and mountain ranges such as the Swiss Alps — hence the name.

The Donington dual-purpose body was introduced in 1958; this was one of a number of important events this year. The body featured a single-piece coach door ahead of the front axle, a high waist-rail and window line with small bus style glazing having top sliding ventilators the norm. The body was to a maximum length of 33ft and would usually seat around 41 passengers often on an AEC Reliance or Leyland Tiger Cub chassis. A restyle in the early 1960s introduced larger window bays that were deeper and larger to make five side window bays instead of the fussy seven small ones. This no doubt made the interior less claustrophobic.

In a second significant event in 1958, Duple bought the long-standing company of Willowbrook Ltd, Loughborough. Duple carried on building its BET-style single-deckers, fairly basic coach bodies and some double-deckers.

Thirdly in 1958, Duple bodied the small capacity Bedford C521 chassis. This was the successor to the OB but with forward-control steering and would later be redesignated the VAS.

Finally in 1958, the Ford Motor Co launched a chassis to vie for the Bedford SB's customers. Marketed as the 570E, Duple built a body for it called Yeoman, which could seat 41 passengers in its 33ft length. Although it shared many common body parts with the Super Vega, it had a differently styled front with a softer edged windscreen, a barred front grille; it usually carried the name Thames on its front, by which Ford Commercial Vehicles were known as until the mid-1960s.

These two coaches illustrate the changes to the rear end of the Super Vega of the period between 1959 and 1962, on the left, with that of the Vega from the mid-1950s. Both vehicles were based upon the Bedford SB with seating capacity unaltered over the period.

This very handsome and spotless coach was photographed in London, having travelled from Litcham, near Dereham, in Norfolk. The chassis beneath was a Commer Avenger with a TS3 two-stroke engine. This resulted in the vehicle being very noisy in comparison to other marques although a brisk performer on long journeys. Duple built a taller body for the Commer so that the engine could be fully under the floor, eliminating the raised cover between the driver and front passengers or courier. This style of body was the Corinthian. *G R Mills*

This is an official Duple photograph that portrays a 33ft-long Donington body on, probably, a short wheelbase AEC Reliance chassis. This body style was more of a Spartan, dual-purpose version of the Britannia in most cases. This coach was built as a luxurious 41-seater with very well spaced seats, smart brightwork and wheel trims. The dipping side trim does not fit the modern straight waist rail, however. Glazed cover panels and mesh luggage racks let the sunshine through whilst eight slider window vents kept the saloon well ventilated.

Dated November 1958, this is an official view of a Bedford SB chassis fitted with a Duple Super Vega coach body.

66 *I'm looking for an eye-opener, Bill, something different . . . advanced design, top-flight interior comfort — a real prestige job.* 99

66 *Same here, Harry, except that as a smaller operator, I must watch the pennies . . . downright economy for me . . . plus reliability. Now there's a Duple coach . . .* 99

Cue for both to plump for the coach with all these qualities—the new Bedford-Duple Super-Vega... the coach you can run at really competitive prices.

NEW SUPER-VEGA
— 41-passenger luxury touring coach. Full details from your Bedford dealer.

Duple Motor Bodies Limited, The Hyde, Hendon, London, N.W.9. COLindale 6412
Repair and Service facilities available at Midland Factory
Swingbridge Road, Loughborough. (Loughborough 4541).

An advert for the new Super Vega from *Bus & Coach* for February 1959.

Developments in the 1960s

Duple acquired a major rival in H V Burlingham of Blackpool during 1960 and soon afterwards this business was renamed Duple (Northern). Burlingham was renowned for building high quality bodies on mostly heavyweight chassis. Handsome half-cab coaches had been succeeded in 1950 by the centre-entrance, underfloor-engined Seagull body. A very popular purchase for a decade, very few designs had the Seagull's presence or style.

Unfortunately, when Duple acquired Burlingham, the Blackpool outfit was producing much less attractive designs than had gone before. Its large body — the Seagull 70 — bore no resemblance to the original and appeared to be a clone of the Harrington Cavalier, mimicking the latter's curved waist-rail, stepped window line and short window bay behind the driver's cab and front entrance. The obvious difference was at the front and rear. The back window and windscreen were both divided by a thick pillar, whilst below the windscreen was a fairly crude arrangement of chromium, twin headlights and moulded fins — no doubt inspired by American cars of this period.

This is a Duple Yeoman body fitted to a Ford Thames 570E chassis and dated originally from late 1960. Although registered in Surrey, presumably by a dealer, the coach was originally operated by a company in west Wales.

Pictured in the livery of Western Welsh, this is a May 1963 Leyland Leopard fitted with a Duple Alpine Continental body. It passed to Black & White Motorways of Cheltenham in 1971; subsequently operated by Wessex National and Creamline, before passing to the scrapyard in late 1979.

The outstanding DUPLE-A.E.C. BRITANNIA as supplied to Samuelsons New Transport Ltd.

"TO BE HONEST...

...When I buy my coaches they have got to be rather special. As an established operator I know what competition I'm up against. I need a coach that looks good. One that immediately impresses my passengers — and gives them confidence. I want them to know from the moment they look at the coach that they're in for a really comfortable ride. It must be good for the driver, too. He wants every modern aid to safety, so do the passengers — so do I! It's got to be economical, and—but need I say more? When I want coaches, I want Duple! Mine are Britannias."

DUPLE MOTOR BODIES LIMITED

THE HYDE, HENDON, LONDON, N.W.9. TEL: COLINDALE 6412

Repair and Service also at Duple Group Factories: Willowbrook Limited, Derby Road, Loughborough. Tel: 5602
Duple Motor Bodies (Midland) Ltd., Swingbridge Road, Loughborough. Tel: 4841.

This advert for the Duple AEC Britannia portrayed a coach supplied to Samuelsons New Transport Ltd, a London-based operator, was published in *Bus & Coach* during November 1960.

The Seagull 61 catered for the smaller operator who bought the 33ft chassis from Bedford and Ford. This body and the Seagull 70 featured a unique idea in having the centre of its roof raised above the aisle between the seats. Curved Perspex panels ran the length of the coach to achieve this. Although practical in allowing more headroom along the vehicle, the visual aspect was as unpleasant as the rest of its looks.

A pair of new coach designs built at the Blackpool factory appeared during 1961. Firstly, the Firefly had an appearance totally different to the Super Vega, with deeper windows and deeper sliding vents. The roof was shallow and tapered down towards the rear end, but the body had a straight waist-rail and bottom edge to the windows. The front end featured a single-piece windscreen with wrap-round glazed corners, which were divided with their polished pillars. Below this sat a horizontally barred grille flanked by twin headlights in a metal surround.

The second new model, the Dragonfly, was larger and designed for the heavyweight chassis although it included all of the Firefly's styling traits. Neither of these designs was hugely successful for Duple and, in fact, only six examples of the Dragonfly were

Pictured waiting at a bus stop, this small coach was a Duple Compact built on the petrol-engined Bedford J2 chassis. The body was Spartan at best and not very attractive compared to the Super Vegas of the time. A maximum of 19 seats could fit into its basic shell but the body was narrow and consequently so were the passenger seats. The widest seats were those provided for the driver and courier — above the front axle — with the engine cover and gear lever between them. The coach is in the orange livery of House's of Watlington and dated from the early 1960s.

built. Yet again ideas from 'across the pond' appeared to influence these body styles. They may well have suited the oil wells of Texas and casinos in Las Vegas, but they did not relate to the British coach operator and poor order books told the story.

In a further attempt to satisfy previous Burlingham customers, the Gannet was unveiled by Duple for the 1962 season. This was a body of 41-seat capacity and outwardly appeared a clone of the Yeates' body styles with pleasing lines to the side and rear end and covered spats over the rear wheel arches. Unfortunately, the front end was horrid, with a three-piece windscreen of severely angular proportions that was shallower than the side glazing, resulting in disjointed lines and too much metalwork below the screen. This was a melange of angles, fins and chromed shapes of various sorts — in a word: horrendous! This was the final body style to carry a Burlingham badge.

Luckily Duple had some better ideas in 1962 with the announcement of the Bella range of bodies. Early versions had fussy side mouldings that helped the use of

This very well kept Bedford SB/Duple, then owned by John H. Sims, shows the style of body that evolved from the classic Butterfly Grille model. A keen eye can spot huge similarities with the larger Britannia bodies. Although in a minority, the author preferred this design of all the SB/Duple varieties.

This little coach body, aptly named the Compact, was designed and built to be fitted exclusively to the Bedford J2 chassis and seated 19 but only sold in small numbers. The petrol-engined coach had a limited market and Plaxton reduced its Embassy body to fit the J2 with more success. The Embassy was taller with deeper windows and seemed more coach-like for the passengers but had a tendency to see the brakes overheat as a result of the wheels being cocooned and so were less well ventilated.

three or more colours in a livery, but as the 1960s progressed the bright work became more uniform, straighter and frankly boring in comparison.

The Bedford VAS 29-seater carried a body named Bella Vista and the larger, more popular Bedford SB carried the Bella Vega body. To complete the larger Bedford line-up, a 36ft body named the Vega Major was developed for the then new and cutting edge twin-steer VAL chassis in 1963.

The Bella family of bodies featured a raked back window pillar above the rear wheel arches that broke the monotony of straight, slim pillars and top-sliding vents. Due to the VAL featuring small diameter 16in wheels, the Vega Major always had a top-heavy look as did rival Plaxton's equivalent — the Consort — and from 1965 the new Panorama.

The Vega Major survived in production until 1967 after a short-lived restyle the previous season, but the relatively new Panorama from Plaxton was more modern and winning more orders.

Other bodies of the Bella range were given names and dedicated to a particular chassis. Ford chassis had seen an increase in sales for its 570E Trader, which

New to Crimson Tours of St Ives, Cornwall, in 1962 this superb Bedford SB3/Super Vega is a wonderful survivor of its type. The vehicle is fitted with a petrol engine and the body accommodates 41 passengers. The vehicle spent many years with Bird of Hunstanton, West Norfolk, and was bought straight out of service for preservation by Len Wright.

competed directly with the SB from Bedford. Visually similar to the Bella Vega, Duple called the bodywork for the Ford chassis the Trooper.

When Ford introduced its first 36ft chassis in late 1963, Duple's body for it was named the Marauder — a rather menacing title for a welcoming coach trip! As with the Bella Vega versus the Trooper, it was difficult to distinguish a Marauder body from the Duple Commodore, but the location of maintenance flaps along the bodywork varied from chassis to chassis, so was often a good pointer to what was underneath.

In general, Ford's products never achieved the longevity of Bedford's more sedate, lower revving models and the author has yet to locate a Marauder or Trooper that survived long enough to be preserved. If any reader can correct him with some encouraging news, please get in touch through the publisher.

A completely new design was introduced in 1962: the Alpine Continental. This body was like nothing else from the Duple stable, having very flat sides, a choice of short length windows with slider ventilation or larger, single-piece bays for a much cleaner appearance. The stepped waistline just aft of the front axle made it stand out from the crowd, the window pillar above this feature was sloped forwards in contrast to nearly all Duple designs that raked backwards above the rear axle. The body certainly looked as if its origins lay abroad and closely resembled coachwork from

Produced by AEC and featuring the new 36ft-long Reliance chassis, this advert from *Bus & Coach* in April 1962 showed the model fitted with a Duple Continental body.

In September 1962, Bedford launched its VAL twin-steer chassis. Undergoing pre-production tests, one of the early examples is seen fitted with a Duple Vega Major 52-seat body. Duple was one of a number of manufacturers to supply bodies for the chassis.

Belgium and Holland but Duple was confident enough in this style to introduce a second variant. Known simply as the Continental, this only really differed from the Alpine version in its lower frontal treatment, which featured a twin headlamp unit either side of the grille that tapered inwards as it reached bumper level, but the top and bottom of the grille was straight edged and sat neatly below the mid-height trim.

The Alpine Continental on the other hand carried two front cooling grilles at bumper level, with a spotlight inset in each of them. These grilles often curved upwards towards

A double rarity is recorded here, especially as it comes from a large operator. This is a Duple Firefly body, with a capacity of 41 seated, fitted to a Ford Thames 570E chassis on vehicle supplied to Wallace Arnold. The styling was very different to the Super Vega, with a straight waist-rail and side trim albeit with a gentle drop towards the rear. The look was late 1950s America: covered wheels and lots of glass with fins and angles. The shallow roof dipped towards the rear to meet a wrap-around three-piece rear window. In the author's opinion, with a more attractive front, this model could have outsold the Plaxton Consort/Embassy.

the centre and above were two headlamps either side, recessed in the glass fibre panel. This curve to the middle formed a protruding brow above the headlights, and the author often thought it looked frog-like from photographs he had studied. Triumph built a sports car that had the same effect and named it the Frog-eye Sprite!

Both bodies used a single-piece curved windscreen and, unusually, a marker light was fitted either side below this. These bodies only achieved limited success and were quietly dropped from production after about five years.

A more conventional, staid design — called the Commodore — also first appeared in 1962. Built for the 33ft heavyweight chassis with an underfloor engine — the established AEC Reliance or increasingly popular Leyland Leopard in most cases. Early examples borrowed the sloping windows pillars from the Bella Vega range as well as the curved, deep front grille. The body evolved to get panoramic glazing and a newly designed grille for 1966; this would also go on to grace other Bella style bodies, but not the Bedford SB, Bella Vega.

Duple's product range was very strong despite the Continental's failure and the earlier setbacks of the Dragonfly, Firefly and Gannet models. The Bella family of bodies was still popular and, when Duple bought the body-building business of W S Yeates, Loughborough, in 1963, another competitor was eradicated from the market place.

Yeates' bodies were in the main very ornate; the early Europa bodies of the 1950s had much bright-work all round and often spats over their rear wheels. The

25

company also built bus bodies that appeared to be less basic than other suppliers' offerings. Some operators preferred Yeates as the company quite happily tailored its build to please customer requests.

The Delaine — a well-respected operator from Bourne, Lincolnshire — chose Yeates a number of times for bus and coach orders. Once Duple had absorbed W S Yeates, Willowbrook — under the Duple umbrella but still a separate entity — carried out the double-deck orders Duple received. The Delaine carried on buying from Duple up to the late 1980s, operating some very smart Leyland Tigers with Dominant single-deck bus bodywork, still lined out in the traditional way with beading along the sides and polished wheel hubs.

The Commander body was introduced in 1964 and offered 33ft and 36ft lengths on an AEC or Leyland chassis. Large, panoramic windows mimicked the rival Plaxton body of this size, the Panorama. Duple supplied a similar body for the front-engined Ford 676E chassis, and named it the Mariner. This chassis was the forerunner of the Ford R226 that became a well-liked lightweight buy until superseded by the R1114.

Bedford introduced its own forward-entrance, 45-seat PSV chassis in 1965 — the VAM — which was a direct result of Vauxhall Motors having its hand forced into action.

Before Duple acquired W S Yeates, the Loughborough concern had been developing and later re-engineering the existing Bedford SB chassis to feature an entrance ahead of the front axle and increased seating capacity. The project, named FE44 (front entrance; 44 seats), encouraged a number of operators into

An official Vauxhall photograph recording a Duple Vega 41-seat body fitted to a Bedford SB chassis in September 1964.

Recorded at a Bedford inspired rally held at Huntingdon racecourse, this is a Bedford VAM5 fitted with a Venture body. The vehicle was supplied new to Myalls of Bassingbourn in 1966 and the company subsequently repurchased it in order to restore it to original condition. The VAM featured a front entrance and larger engine choices when introduced.

placing orders. Yeates moved the front axle back to allow for an entrance and step well beside the front engine.

After periods of use in service, some FE44s developed structural problems in the Yeates' bodywork; this is thought to have been caused by the original SB chassis not coping with the extra weight and stress at the front.

Complaints to Vauxhall/Bedford could not be acted upon, as Yeates did the conversion work without the manufacturer's blessing. This did, however, make Bedford realise that a market for a similar chassis existed, and the VAM was its response. Duple built a new body — the Bella Venture — for the VAM chassis. Three engine options were offered: a Bedford petrol or diesel unit or, thirdly, a Leyland 0.400 diesel engine.

The Bella Venture appeared a nicely balanced coach body and first appeared for the 1966 season. Deep windows with slider ventilation and glazed core panels were an option that gave a light, airy feel and the VAM's bigger wheels made it look less top-heavy than the larger Bedford VAL/Vega Major on its 16in wheels. Side trim was generally being simplified during the 1960s and the Bella Venture carried straight beading that gave a nice deep skirt from headlights to rear lights. A shallow flash ran horizontally from front corners to the rear, these having angled ends and helping to vary a livery, the waistline curved downwards gently approaching the back, like other Bella designs before it.

Oddly the body names appeared rather confusing — on one hand you had the Bella Vega, Vista and Venture that encouraged the idea of open views, adventure and maybe foreign travel — whilst, on the other, the bodies for the heavy-weights — generally more capable of touring and distance travel — continued with names associated with the British empire and the military, such as the Commander, Commodore and Viscount.

Dating originally to 1959, this Bedford SB3 is fitted with a Duple Super Vega C41F body. Now owned, following an expensive professional restoration, by the Norfolk-based company Sidelines Coaches of Long Stratton, WLO 685 can be seen regularly across the county. The Super Vega body shown here differed little from the Yeoman body fitted to the contemporary Ford Thames.

Duple had a rather over-loaded model range by the mid-1960s compared to its main rival, Plaxton, although the Scarborough firm did introduce modern titles to enthuse the coach buyer. The Panorama ousted the Consort, but the Embassy carried on to be supplied on the Bedford SB chassis, and lasted even longer on the Bedford J2 20-seater — the last examples being registered in 1972-73.

In England's one and only football world cup winning year — 1966 — Duple broke new ground to launch its new Viceroy body at that year's Commercial Motor Show. The new design lacked the curves of previous models, the body sides being almost flat, only tapering in (still at an angle) where the large side windows mated up to the slider vents above. The only curves of note belonged to the grille sides, headlights and wheels!

Side trim on the Viceroy was straight as was the waist-rail, only broken by a kick-up mid-height to correspond with a window pillar angled forward behind the first window bay. This style of shorter first side bay had become popular in the early 1960s for the coachbuilders Thomas Harrington of Hove, Sussex. Its Cavalier and Grenadier bodies were very stylish and sold well, replaced by the handsome Legionnaire in 1964, Harrington left a major hole in the coach market when construction ceased in 1965 very abruptly. In the author's opinion, the Legionnaire was ahead of its time by about 10 years, and a company with that foresight was a sad loss to the industry.

The Duple Viceroy windscreen was wider at the lower edges, wrapping round the corner pillars to the sides. This was almost reversed at the back end were the top edges were wider to fit the sloping corner pillars. The Viceroy was nicely finished off with straight edged skirts.

A revamp of the model in 1968 introduced a full-width, rectangular grille, front and rear bumpers were not so hefty and featured matt black corner pieces married to a chromium middle section. Really noticeable were twin headlights recessed into

Undated, but probably originating in the late 1960s, this official view records a standard 11m BET-style single-deck dual-purpose body fitted to a AEC Reliance chassis. The vehicle was supplied with panoramic windows and luxury coach seats complete with antimacassars.

the front behind glass covers; these sat in a full-length, wrap-round band of aluminium trim, ribbed horizontally. This sat just above the slim bumpers and also included the rear light clusters. Beneath these modifications the lower edges of the body were given rounded-off skirts that did not fit well with the Viceroys angles.

Over six years of production until late 1972, the Viceroy lost market share to the Panorama — a more modern design from its introduction and more effortless to update in order to stay ahead. With Duple being left in Plaxton's wake, worse was to come with continental coachbuilders poised to enter the mainstream coach market as the 1970s approached.

PSV dealer Alf Moseley began importing a stylish and inviting body on the Bedford VAM chassis in 1969. The builder was Salvador Ceatano with a model named the Cascais. The new contender was modern, finished very nicely inside and out, and aged the Duple products at a stroke.

Viceroy 36

This is the longer 52 seat version of the dramatically attractive new Viceroy styling, designed for mounting on the Ford R226 or Bedford VAL chassis.

Superbly engineered construction with metal underframe, metal pillars, stainless steel pillar cappings.

Greatly increased window area with new high-level sliding lights.

More luxurious seating than ever with brilliantly styled new interior decor.

Fluorescent lighting and illuminated rear name panel are basic items.

45 seat versions are also available on Ford R192 and Bedford VAM chassis.

See the Duple Group Exhibits at the International Commercial Motor Transport Exhibition, Stands Nos. 38, 39, 40, 47, 55, 57. Earls Court, Sept 29—Oct 1, 1966.

An advert from September 1966 promoting the new Viceroy 36 52-seat body suitable for the Ford R226 or, as illustrated, the Bedford VAL.

Into the 1970s

Although the Viceroy was the body for Bedford and Ford's larger models, the Commander remained available until around 1970 as the choice for AEC, Leyland and Bristol products. Heavyweight, powerful and robust coaches were increasingly needed as Britain's road network grew and longer express routes became more widespread. The Leyland Leopard and AEC Reliance led this market from the early 1960s and were the only real mainstream choice of chassis until foreign manufactures attacked the market from the mid-1970s.

A third choice — the Bristol RELH bodied with the Commander — had sold in very small numbers to the Tilling group of companies — the ancestors of the National Bus Company.

Behind the scenes, Duple was undergoing structural changes in the late 1960s. It was decided to close the Hendon factory and offices, relocating the work to Duple (Northern) at Blackpool, the old Burlingham premises. This brought to a close nearly 45 years of body-building at Hendon. Soon after this the company was taken over by George Hughes and Frank Ford.

From the early 1970s, Duple built the Viceroy — a heavyweight product — ending the Commander range in effect. The Bedford SB and VAS chassis received restyled Duple bodies from 1970; these were called the Vega 31 and Vista respectively. In appearance, they were an amalgam of Viceroy grille, bumpers and front peaked dome in a smaller Commander body — so the look lived on in part. The shallow glazing, curved cove panels (roof sides) and screens front and rear were pure Commander.

A late development in the Viceroy's life was an express version that qualified for the then Bus Grant funding scheme. The 10m body was supplied on either the Bedford YRQ (successor to the VAM) or the Ford R192 chassis. A condition of the grant meant the in-swing Viceroy entrance had to be widened so that, when completed, it gave the coach a two-piece folding door. This resulted in the front corner pillars being more upright, with the result that the usual angled Viceroy windscreen could not be used. The screen used with the Vega 31 and Bella style bodies of the past was installed above the front radiator to mate up nicely to the pillars and body sides. The windscreen was two-piece with a central divide on all Viceroy Express models.

The body was also gained a new profile to its roof-line; the semi-stage carriage work that the Express was designed for required a front destination display above the windscreen. The Viceroy in its normal guise featured a gentle slope of its roof to the front with a shallow peak above the screen; this would not accommodate a display of decent size. A larger route display unit on the Express levelled off out the

This 36ft-long Duple Viceroy 37 body was fitted to a three-axle Bedford VAL in 1971. The body was supplied long before legislation required vehicles to be strengthened to cope with possible roll-overs. In 1971, slim window pillars, a shallow roof and a vast amount of glass were the orders of the day. No doubt, the passengers appreciated the top slider vents in preventing the saloon overheating in hot weather.

This was the very first brand new coach acquired by the Diss, Norfolk, based R W Chenery when supplied in 1972. It's a Duple 45-seat Viceroy body fitted to a Bedford YRQ chassis. The chassis differed from the VAM model it replaced in having the engine under the floor between the axles rather than under a large cover at the front of the coach.

Pictured when only a few weeks old, this very neat Duple body was fitted to a Bedford YRQ chassis. The 45-seat body carried a two-leaf entrance door to qualify for the bus grant funding of the time. The style was the Viceroy Express, the final and neatest version of the Viceroy family. Its more upright frontal aspect suited the modern flatter sides. *G R Mills*

roof-line to the front and almost accidentally produced the neatest, most modern Viceroy of them all. This was an excellent finale for the design prior to bowing out of production in late 1972.

Duple sold the business of Willowbrook, Loughborough, in 1971 to George Hughes as a going concern. The following year saw the death of Duple's founder, Herbert White; he was aged 94 and had overseen some fantastic achievements and changes in his time. Duple itself was sold on again in 1972 to the Cranleigh Group, a Manchester based industrial holdings company. Frank Ford carried on as Executive Chairman of Duple Coachbuilders Ltd and continued bringing the company back into profit and increased production; he had taken over a loss making concern in 1970.

The same year, 1972, also saw the announcement of a completely new coach body, launched at that year's Commercial Motor Show. This brand-new range would be a direct assault on Plaxton; the latter's market leading Panorama body had evolved into the Panorama Elite and was making Duple's offerings appear ancient and old hat.

Mindful of this, designers and management developed the Dominant range to grace all chassis from the 29-seat Bedford VAS to a 12m coach that would carry 57 passengers.

Orders from most British operators of the time were for either 10m or 11m coaches. There were four main window bays on the 10m Dominant, four and a half

This is a classic coach from the mid-1970s. It is a Leyland Leopard PSU4R 11m (36ft) chassis fitted with a Duple Dominant 1 C51F body and is seen in the livery of Bassett's Coachways of Tittensor, Stoke-on-Trent. The coach was new to W Robinson & Sons (Great Harwood) Ltd in 1976 and passed to Bassett's five years later. The coach is at the time of writing undergoing a full restoration by a member of the Potteries Omnibus Preservation Society.

To Duple's credit, this Leyland Leopard was an attractive coach when pictured at Blackpool. The National Bus Company ordered many from the company during the 1970s. The vehicles were normally painted in the drab corporate all-over white livery. This looked crisp when new but once in service, the rain-soaked road and motorways soon took their toll, resulting in vehicles that looked dirty and scruffy.

This view, dating to the mid-1970s, shows the interior of a Dominant I body fitted to a Ford chassis — the engine cover is the giveaway. The dashboard surround has a straight top edge, which replaced the larger, curved original.

Taken in strong sunshine at the Blackpool Works, this vehicle was part of a batch supplied to Nottingham City Transport. It entered service in March 1976 and was a Dominant E-type body fitted on a Leyland Leopard 11m chassis. In essence, the vehicle had bus fittings in a coach bodyshell. This rear view clearly depicts the lack of brightwork. Although complete, it looks almost unfinished — no trim around the wheel arches, nothing on the rear and just a single trim strip on the sides. There was no forced ventilation; hence no pods on the roof and the six slider vent windows aired the saloon. At least two of the batch survive in preservation at the time of writing.

on the 11m. The glazing was formed of deep, single-piece, bays with narrow pillars between them. Below these a full length, deep, horizontally ribbed section of chrome trim ran. This incorporated forward indicator repeaters and more along the body if specified. Top, slider ventilation of the windows could also be supplied. The Panorama now had serious competition for its crown.

The frontal treatment of the new Dominant was much tidier than previous Duple products. A gently curved, two-piece windscreen shared its upper and lower edges with the levels of the side windows. Twin circular headlights flanked a simply barred, shallow central grille and indicator/sidelights and screen. Depending on the chassis and its cooling system, some Dominant bodies needed extra ventilation in their front panel. This meant that destination displays or illuminated name panels would be fitted above the windscreen. Plaxton had done this on the Panorama and, because of the chassis that required the modification, it became known in the industry as the Bristol Dome.

Large fleets are important, sometimes vital, for a coachbuilder's future. Duple had been supplying Wallace Arnold of Leeds with coach bodies as far back as the era of the Bedford OB. The relationship came to an end during 1987 with the delivery of the final Volvo B10M/Duple 340s. Dating from 10 years earlier, this and the adjacent vehicle were both 11m Leyland Leopards fitted with Dominant 2 bodywork. The colour scheme was cream, grey and orange.

The new Dominant became an instant success for Duple, with independent operators and larger concerns, including the then recently formed National Bus Company, which took large numbers for its various local subsidiaries. These were mostly mounted on 11m Leyland Leopards, working on cross-country and National Express routes.

For the smaller operator, Duple grafted the Dominant onto the Bedford VAS and 41-seat SB. These still had their entrance behind the front axle — the old-fashioned way — but nevertheless sold in small numbers until Bedford ceased chassis building.

Another major customer for the Dominant was W Alexander, part of the Scottish Bus Group with subsidiaries called Fife, Midland and Northern. During a period of about three years, Ford's R1014 chassis became a well-liked chassis for a frugal, lightweight 45-seat coach to be used in local and middle-distance stage service and private hire. The Bus Grant also covered Scotland and most Dominants had two-piece doors and the wider entrance required for this subsidy. Ford at this time had its front-mounted engine under a sizeable padded cover beside the driver, so the wider entrance and step-well made for easier loading and existing.

This is an official Duple photograph taken outside the Blackpool factory and shows a Dominant 2 body fitted on to an 11m Bedford YMT. The vehicle was delivered new to Hill of Tredegar in South Wales in 1977/78. It was to be last Duple-bodied vehicle supplied to the operator; future orders went to Plaxton. It was sold in February 1983 to Williams of Cwmdu, spending some nine years with that operator.

A service bus body was unveiled in 1974 that had a family resemblance to its coach brother. The Dominant bus body was built on all the popular chassis of the 1970s, apart from the mid-engined DAF. Lightweight Fords and Bedfords were hugely popular and heavyweights from AEC — the trusty Reliance — the Leyland Leopard and the reputation building Volvo B58 all carried the bus body. These three products could all be built to the maximum 12m length. The body had deep side windows for good vision and give a light feel to the interior. It lacked the bright-work of the coach body, but smart beading was employed to line the body out nicely. The roof cove panels were angled inwards rather than curved, as was the norm in the mid-1970s. A deep destination display sat above a curved BET-style screen.

In 1975 a collaboration between Duple and Bedford GM produced a prototype/one-off coach named the Dominant Goldliner. Bedford had just up-rated its 466cc and introduced this as the YMT chassis. It was hoped by Bedford that a better middle/long-distance product had been achieved, so Duple were asked to build a more motorway derived body-style. The Dominant body was highlighted to accommodate a higher saloon floor and the coach taken to Marrakesh for trials and distance running in hot conditions and on roads of various states of repair. The road tests were published in *Commercial Motor* magazine.

Owned by Lodge's Coaches of High Easter, Essex, since new in 1978, this is a 53-seat Duple Dominant 2 fitted to an 11M Bedford YMT chassis. This shows the effect of Michelotti's redesign upon the original body. The polished chromium above the lower band of blue indicates the floor level.

This handsome vehicle remained unique; road testing it in areas and conditions for which it was not designed seemed fool-hardy at best, putting extra load on the ventilation system in the coach and the cooling of the mid-engined chassis. Moreover foreign countries were not exactly over-loaded with Duple engineers able to sort out a wholly British product. This new machine was intended to travel Barnsley to Birmingham on trunk roads and motorways not Morocco to Mali on dirt road and desert!

Duple's main rival Plaxton discontinued the Panorama Elite range in 1975, introducing a completely new design — the Supreme. It first appeared on the small Bedford VAS, the larger SB and Bristol's mid-coach chassis, the LHS. Full size products from Bedford, Ford, AEC, Leyland and Seddon all carried Supreme coachwork from 1976.

Duple, not wanting to be left behind again, asked Italian designer Giovanni Michelotti to give the Dominant a restyle. His ideas resulted in the Dominant 2 that first appeared in 1976 on the R-suffix registration plate. The deep side windows were still used but the stand-out changes were at the front and back. A much deeper windscreen was used, which lined up with the lower edge of the ribbed trim still in place below the side windows. To match up, the driver's window was made

Two-piece grant doors are fitted to this 1979 C53F Dominant 2 recorded at Sea Palling, Norfolk. Brian Wiltshire mostly operated Bedford coaches and, latterly, had a preference for DAFs so this AEC Reliance was an unusual buy. It was originally new to Eynon of Trimsaran in Wales.

This Bedford YLQ/Dominant 2 features tinted glazing, polished wheel trims, lots of chrome and an excellent paint finish. The 45-seat vehicle was delivered new to Cyril Kenzie, moving to Porter, Great Totham, before passing to Andrew Fowler of Fowlers Travel. The coach, at the time of writing, now belongs to Norfolk Coachways.

deeper and, oddly but helpfully, the entrance door glazing was this light on the Dominant 1, so needed no alteration. A larger kerb window in the lower part of the one-piece door was now standard.

The deep windscreen gave terrific forward vision for driver and passengers alike and, from the outside, the whole black moulded instrument binnacle could be seen ahead of the steering wheel. Below the screen, a shallow front dash panel discarded the circular twin headlights and in their place were flush fitting twin rectangular units, with a new indicator/sidelight unit on the outside of this. This left very little space for a radiator grille, resulting in an almost anonymous area between the headlights, which only looked interesting when a chassis builder's motif or name was applied.

Michelotti also decided to square off the lower panel skirt edges, which vastly improved the side appearance. The original Viceroy featured this and looked much neater than the Viceroy 2 with its rounded off skirts. Unfortunately the original Dominant inherited these when first introduced in 1972.

A lucky find when recorded at Great Yarmouth Coach Park in the 1990s as it was rare to photograph a Duple Dominant 3, even when new, as they were the least popular of all the Dominant styles. This coach was based around a Bedford YNT chassis and was originally supplied to Reliance of Newbury in April 1981. This well-presented example shows to good effect the shallow trapezoid windows and how they heighten the waist-line, despite being no taller than other versions of the Dominant body.

Based some seven miles from the author's home in Norfolk, Neaves Coaches provided transport to and from school for him in the 1980s. This recently repainted Bedford YNT fitted with a Duple Dominant 4 body was originally registered in Preston.

A rare beast recorded at Great Yarmouth. This is a Bova/Duple Calypso. The vehicle's low height and Caribbean windscreen and side glazing made for a strange blend with its apparent high ground clearance. A straight 53-seat body, integrally built, it belonged to Towler, Emneth, Wisbech in Cambridgeshire when photographed.

The Dominant 2 also had its rear end reworked. A new flat, shallower rear window sat higher on the body and showed less of the back-row five seats, and avoided the sunlight fading them. Below this was usually an illuminated panel above a chrome trim strip that fed across the rear to mate up with the trim beneath its side windows. The rear lights were now neat horizontal units, but oblong clusters either side of the boot-lid could be specified. NBC and large fleet orders often preferred this plainer option.

The Dominant 2 got new bumpers front and back of a much sturdier design. The original Dominant had carried the slim style bumpers of the Viceroy it replaced. A recess was incorporated in the new bumpers to accommodate front/rear registration plates and a rubber step directly above the registration number plate aided cleaning of the large windscreen, with a convenient grab handle fitted to the screen dividing strip — all windscreens being two-piece.

To satisfy more conservative buyers, the Dominant 1 was given a facelift to attract the large fleet operators, often NBC companies or municipal concerns wanting trusty, simple Leyland Leopards. Quite a large number were also sold over the border in Scotland to the Scottish Bus Group, again mostly on Leopards.

Due to its radiator position, the Dominant 2 could not be adapted to fit the Bedford VAS or SB, so the revised Dominant 1 would continue to be offered until 1986 when chassis supply ended.

Finished to a beautiful standard, this coach dated from January 1980 and was bought by Cyril Kenzie of Shepreth in Cambridgeshire. Volvo chassis became a firm favourite for the operator's executive vehicles. This Volvo B58 chassis is fitted with a 57-seats 12m tint-glazed Dominant 2 body.

The Final Decade

After being the flagship model for four years, in 1980 Duple extended the Dominant range by adding variants 3 and 4. Plaxton had updated their Supreme the previous year and the resulting Supreme IV was much tidier and won many orders at the time. The new models were hoped to claw some business back to Blackpool again.

Duple's first salvo of the offensive brought in a radical styling change for the Dominant. The side windows of the Mk3 variant were trapezoid shaped and very shallow compared to the glazing used by other builders. The idea had been taken from the Alexander M-type body introduced in 1986 for Scottish long distance express routes. Alexander appeared to get its inspiration from American Greyhound coaches. Small, high set windows and ribbed side sections were pure Uncle Sam of the early 1960s.

The front and rear end stayed basically the same as Duple's Dominant 2, but the larger bumpers were ousted in favour of thick rubber strip inlaid with beading. These flowed around the corners to the wheel arches. The driver's window and front entrance glazing did not line up with the side bays at all and, when fitted with a shallower Dominant 1 screen, looked very awkward and an obvious mix-up of parts.

Luckily Duple's Mk 4 design was more conventional and more of a subtle rework of Michellotti's ideas. The deep original side windows were made shallower to give a higher waist-rail and, like the Dominant 3, gave the impression of a higher floor in the coach. The under window chrome trim was simplified on both versions and new rear light clusters, which protruded out slightly to a subtle angle, were fitted.

Both bodies could be built on products from Bedford, Ford, Leyland and Volvo; the Dominant 4 was built on a DAF MB200DKTL 12m chassis for the first time in 1980. Very few of either body were built at the shorter 10m length, but 11m and 12m versions were popular purchases. A small market still existed for the shorter 8.5m 35-seat coach and a Dominant 4 body was produced for Ford and Bedford customers during 1982 and 1983.

The Dominant Mk 3 found its biggest customer north of the border in Scotland. The Scottish Bus Group (owners of W Alexander) bought batches on the then new Volvo chassis — the B10M — and Leyland's new air sprung, larger engined, more refined Tiger 245. The latter replaced the trusty, solid but out-dated Leopard chassis. The new coaches were destined for long-distance work across Scotland and down to Birmingham and London, covering the duties Alexander M-types had previously covered.

The bus building activities of Duple received a shot in the arm in the latter part of 1980 with the acquisition of Metal Sections Ltd, Oldbury in the West Midlands. The company was primarily in the business of building completely knocked down

Above: New to the well-known north-eastern independent OK Motor Services of County Durham in May 1981, this vehicle was fitted with a baby Dominant body on to a Bedford VAS5 chassis — the equivalent in the 1980s of the old Duple/OB combination of the 1950s.

Right: Although needing a good exterior clean — it was a crisp but frosty Suffolk Sunday morning — this Bedford YMPS, dating from September 1982, and now owned by Country Travel, was fitted with the baby-sized 8.5m Dominant 2 body seating 35 passengers. The vehicle was originally delivered to M & S W Jarvis of Aberdare.

LIL 5759 demonstrates the original Duple Laser body as fitted to an 11m Bedford YNT. There are obvious similarities between this and the Dominant range. This example was fitted with a single piece windscreen and horizontal wipers, but divided windscreen and upright wipers could also be specified.

(CKD) bodies. In effect, all the parts were manufactured and shipped or flown in kit form in crates across the world to be assembled in their country of operation. This practice had been carried out by body-builders and chassis suppliers for some years, becoming very popular from the 1950s as big players, such as Leyland, became very well liked in export markets like Africa that required simple, reliable and easily maintained lorries and buses. Albion, AEC and Leyland gained an enviable reputation for their reliability and ruggedness in foreign climes.

Much business also came from Asian countries as many Metal Section (Metsec) bodies went to China and Indonesia; these were mostly kits but complete vehicles could also be built at the Oldbury premises. Hong Kong kept ordering Daimler CVG and Guy Arab chassis for their double-deck orders long after both marques were no longer available in Great Britain, so half-cab buses were still plentiful in service during the 1980s. Metsec re-bodied many of these vehicles once the original bodies of various builders had had succumbed to a hard life and very humid, moist temperatures.

A new breed of large capacity double-decker became popular in the late 1980s to move the massive population of the colony. Seating over 100 passengers in a front-entrance, 12m body, the chassis was a three-axle powerful beast based around either

A C35F Dominant 4 body fitted on to a Ford T152 chassis is seen in the livery of Provence Private Hire. The coach was one of a trio originally supplied to Traject of Huddersfield in February and March 1983. It passed to Provence of St Albans in April 1987 via Lovering of Combe Martin. Sold in May 1991, Provence reacquired the coach in September 1992; withdrawn in April 2006, the vehicle survives but is unlicensed.

Right: The Caribbean was Duple's answer to the massive influx of the products from foreign coachbuilders in the mid-1980s. The 49-seat coach was new to Bostocks of Congleton, Cheshire, in April 1983. It is seen here in the livery of DCH Travel at Riverside, Norwich.

Below: Introduced in 1974, the Dominant bus body was manufactured for 13 years. When photographed, this example was owned by Dews of Somersham, Cambridgeshire, but it had been originally delivered to Chambers of Bures, Suffolk, in March 1984. The 63-seat body was fitted to a late Bedford YMT chassis.

a Dennis Condor or Leyland Olympian. Duple Metsec bodied many of these vehicles for operation in Hong Kong in the late 1980s and quite a number found themselves repatriated back to the UK for further use as high capacity school buses.

Features such as full-depth slider windows, common in Asian countries but not legal over here, needed rectifying before use, but once certified these reimported vehicles became really good earners on large school contracts and work/personnel movements. In fact Firstbus was still using them in East Norfolk up until the end of the last decade on these duties. Once Metsec could not supply the market in Hong Kong, Alexander coachbuilders got a larger market share; the Scottish company, like Metsec, had been supplying bodies on new chassis and rebodying existing fleet vehicles for China Motor Bus over a number of years. It rebodied the final Guy Arab built in 1972 with a new two-door body 10 years later.

An official Duple view, this photograph records the original Laser body in its 12m form. This demonstrator was unusual in having a full depth rear emergency door. The rich black paintwork with gold relief produced a stunning coach. For this range and the taller Caribbean, Duple designed its own stylish wheel trims. The chassis was the powerful Volvo B10M. *Duple*

Recorded at Seacroft Chalet Park, Hemsby, in the late 1990s, this was a Bedford YNT/Laser that had been supplied new to Bostocks of Congleton, Cheshire, in August 1984. The 53-seat body incorporates a modified grille and headlight combination; this was a short-lived cosmetic alteration.

Left: Originally supplied to Wood of Barnsley and recorded here in the livery of Charnock of Sheffield, this was a Bedford YNT/Laser 2 combination. The body featured bonded glazing, which gave a sleeker look, along with a redesigned front end and a modernised interior.

Right: Recorded at its Caister-on-Sea, Norfolk, base this was a 1985 Bedford YNV/Laser 2 that was originally delivered to Youngs of Rampton, Cambridgeshire. When newly delivered, the vehicle was used in General Motors' publicity, being displayed at trade shows and making trips to other operators. From Youngs it passed to Keymers of Aylsham, Norfolk, before being sold in 1990 to Leonard and Charles Reynolds. It was to remain with Reynolds until 2002.

Back with the coaches for the domestic market, the Dominant 3 and 4 got a genuine high-floor version made available for the 1981 season. This was known as the Goldliner and could feature a stepped roof-line behind the driver/entrance or have a level roof profile. This was a competitor to the Plaxton Viewmaster, a high-floor Supreme. Both builders were fighting off ever more exotic, executive coaches from Ceatano, Jonckheere, Padane, Mercedes, Smit and Van Hool.

Seen undergoing a tilt test at the Blackpool factory is an original style Caribbean. The design looked modern and was not dissimilar to the contemporary product from Van Hool: the Alizée model. However, later models lost ground and many sales to Duple's Belgian competitor. The Gastonia-livered coach, one of two supplied by Duple in 1983/84 to the operator, is based upon a Dennis Dorchester mid-engined chassis. *Duple*

Pictured in the livery of Dennis & Trevor Coaches, this is a Caribbean 2 body fitted on to a Leyland Royal Tiger chassis. The vehicle demonstrates the bonded glazing, newly designed front end and flared wheel arches of the model.

The final variation of the Dominant body was a batch of Super Goldliners on the newly developed Dennis Falcon 12m chassis. National Express had requested this combination to be constructed for evaluation as Dennis could deliver their chassis to the Duple factory within a time frame of four months.

Though the Falcon was new to the coach market, it had been derived from an existing 11m single-deck bus chassis. The changes were a higher driving position, air suspension all round and importantly the Gardner engine had been substituted by a turbo-charged V8 Perkins unit. This produced 260bhp and, coupled up to a fully automatic Voith gearbox, gave brisk powerful performance for the Motorway routes National Express Rapide operated in 1982.

The Super Goldliner was in reality a high-floor, executive Dominant 4. The body on the Dennis Falcon had to accommodate a rear engine, so the rear boot-lid was the access point to the Perkins V8; this was flanked at both top corners with hinged flaps for the coolant level and engine stop. Above the disguised boot-lid was a shallow, matt black cooling grille. Duple finished these bodies with matt black lower skirts all-round and the area surrounding the rear windows and long side windows were treated the same way.

The use of black relief vastly improved the long, tall appearance of the bodywork and suited the front curved destination display and surround. This seemed to make the Super Goldliner much more up-to-date than the numerous express coaches with the Bristol Dome of the late 1960s.

This coach in all-over National white would have looked far too bland and made exterior cleaning a nightmare!

The Rapide Falcons were fitted out with 47 reclining seats, centre sunken toilet and a servery. The first of these were delivered in autumn 1982 and were said to have cost £75.000 each at the time.

The final Dominant coaches built to 11m and 12m lengths were registered in 1983 on the then new A-suffix registration plate. A small Dominant 4 remained in build for the 8.5m Bedford YMPS and Ford T152.

Two totally new body styles were announced in 1982. Duple had been reworking the Dominant at regular intervals and really could not alter anything else to keep things fresh. The same problem was also present at Plaxton in Scarborough; its Supreme, introduced in 1975, had undergone mostly cosmetic changes that culminated in the final Supreme VI, visually the worst Supreme built by a distance.

The year 1982 would prove an important one in British coach building as the two 'big players' brought out new ranges to try and stem the popularity of imported coachwork.

Plaxton's answer was the new Paramount range, a completely new body in sizes from 8.5m to the 12m maximum. It was available in standard height format, with a high-floor variant for tours and executive travel. This one range oversaw the end of Supreme and Viewmaster production, the only exception being a smaller version of Supreme IV that survived on the Bedford 29-seat VAS.

This photograph was staged in June 1987 to portray one of the batch of 340/Volvo B10M coaches that had been supplied to Wallace Arnold that year. This high-floor touring coach was by no means Duple's most attractive but the operator's cream and orange livery suits it well. Breaking into supplying the big fleets was very welcome when Duple traditional lightweight market had all but disappeared after Bedford/GM ceased to build suitable chasses in 1986.

The response from Duple was a two-pronged attack. For the customer who wanted a standard height coach used for private hire, contracts or commuter work the new Laser was available in 11m and 12m lengths to suit Bedford, Leyland, DAF and Volvo chassis.

Outwardly this new body displayed origins of Michelotti's ideas. It still carried twin, square flush-fitting headlights with a small barred grille between them; the grille was now of glass fibre and produced in the body colour used. The front panel profile was more raked backwards and, therefore, more aerodynamic than any Dominant had been. The rear end, though more rounded, had definite hints of the Dominant 3 and 4 and carried over the smoother rear light clusters from these models. But unlike previous models, there was no bright-work or trim on the rear of the Laser, just a token rubbing strip around the bumper area.

The side aspect was very smooth and uncluttered on the Laser. A standard exterior trim package featured an aluminium strip below the gasket glazed windows and another at floor level from the front corner to the rear quarter, only broken by the wheel arch top curves.

A nicely posed shot of a 12m Leyland Tiger fitted with a Duple 340 body in service with Alexander Fife. It was in Scottish Citylink's blue, yellow and white livery and was used on express services through Scotland and the rest of the UK. The sloping front roof profile of the body is very evident from this angle.

The roof profile sloped gently downwards at the immediate front, doing away with the fussy peaks and destination domes of the past.

An added feature of the new Laser was a vertical piece of angled flash, set between the drivers window and entrance to divide them from the 4½ bay and 5½ (12m) side windows. Particularly in its 11m form on a simple Bedford YNT chassis, the Laser appeared to be a more rounded and less fussy clone of the Dominant 4, and on the outside there was absolutely nothing wrong in that. The whole coach had a pleasant, clean look and Michelotti's ideas of 1976 were subtly still there.

Despite its good looks, after just one season in build the twin, flush headlights were replaced with single units to allow a wider grille that was finished in polished metal. Apart from aiding frontal cooling, it appeared a purely cosmetic exercise.

The second body to debut for Duple in 1983 was a high-floor coach designed for the executive and holiday tour market; named the Caribbean, it was a hefty, upright body made for heavyweight chassis. This was Blackpool's challenge to the Plaxton Paramount, Caetano Algarve and Van Hool Alizée in the main.

This completely new coach was only offered in the 12m length, and could be powered by DAF, Dennis, Leyland or Volvo chassis. By this time Dennis had abandoned the Falcon as a coach chassis and introduced the mid-engined Dorchester chassis in its place and a few were ordered to power the Caribbean. DAF was still supplying the MB200 chassis, which also had its engine between front and rear axles.

Leyland's trusty, air-sprung Tiger and the market leading Volvo B10M carried the lion's share of Caribbean bodies built. One prototype was constructed on a Neoplan underframe and powered by a Mercedes engine fitted in its rear end; this became unique as the only integral version ever built. Publicity pictures of the time (1984) depict a stylish coach with modern bonded glazing, large luggage locker space as no chassis frame impeded between axles, drivers' sleeping area below the floor, and a very nicely finished interior. A testimony to the engineering and previous custodians of the coach, this one-off still survives at the time of writing, albeit not in use now, but crying out to be preserved forever.

The Caribbean did not sell in the numbers Duple had hoped and the styling tweaks the Laser suffered after one season's build did not do the flagship model any favours visually — the original design was attractive, if a bit heavy-looking. It was obvious in the future, making slight alterations to designs would not keep winning orders against ever stronger competition from foreign builders.

Aside from the major product announcements of 1983, Duple Ltd, Blackpool was bought-out by the Hestair Group in the same year. The most notable name in the Hestair portfolio was Dennis of Guildford, a chassis supplier to Duple since the late 1920s but more famous for the manufacture of fire appliances and municipal vehicles (such as refuse lorries and other special builds). Hestair would steer Duple's business into the choppy waters of survival against a massive increase of imported

The high-floor 340 body was the successor to the Caribbean. This view shows a very new delivery fitted to a DAF SB2300 chassis. It was delivered new in April 1987 and was employed on long-distance express routes in competition with National Express. The 340 body had flared wheel arches and unique wheel trims.

Three brand-new and as yet unregistered coaches await delivery to the Cranborne-based operator Maybury's. The three were Bedford YNV Venturer chassis fitted with Duple 320 55-seat bodies and were registered D446-D448 PGH. The vehicles were delivered to the operator in March 1987. D446 PGH subsequently saw service with Collins of Cambridge.

Left: Recorded at BCA Auctions in Manchester, this Volvo B10M/Duple 340 was a 24-year-old veteran when going under the gavel. The coach had been delivered new to Wallace Arnold. Duple did not have a great deal of success with the 340 range, largely as a result of the increased number of foreign coachbuilders targeting the British market. At the time of writing the coach still survives, in the ownership of Edwards Coach Holidays of South Wales.

Right: Freshly repainted in the livery of Caroline Seagull, Great Yarmouth, when recorded here, this coach was a Bedford YNT fitted with a Duple 320 body. The coach had benefited with being fitted with a replacement Cummins diesel engine and was originally registered D322 GRU in Bournemouth and had previously operated with Scraggs Coaches of Staffordshire. The number plate, at the time of writing, is now affixed to a DAF/Van Hool coach operated by Sanders Coaches of Holt, Norfolk.

coach orders. LAG and Jonckheere of Belguim, Ceatano of Portugal, Berkhof, Van Hool and to a lesser extent Smit and Van Rooijen imported their offerings from Holland, with the Van Hool range becoming hugely popular and breaking into major fleets like Shearings Holidays during 1985.

Mercedes built its own coachwork on its 0303 model; likewise Kässbohrer and Neoplan constructed the bodies for their integral, rear engined coaches. Van Hool and later LAG supplied a good number of integral coaches to fill an increasing market trend.

Another Dutch builder — Bova — had been importing to Britain its high-floor, bulbous looking Futura and the more angular, squared off standard height Europa integral coaches since 1982 and its DAF-powered offerings were winning fans. A Mercedes unit could be specified in the Futura when it first arrived on these shores, but the simple, robust DAF 8.25-litre engine soon became a standard fit.

Though the Futura went from strength to strength, Bova decided its angular Europa had no future and turned to Duple in 1984 to supply an attractive, lowheight body to be engineered as an integral private hire and contract coach. Blackpool had an opportunity to collaborate with its competition to be part of new construction methods and importantly affix their name on them!

The result was the Bova Calypso, an 11m, economical and simple, modern looking coach. Much of its design was borrowed from the taller Caribbean, the bonded side windows deep, square front screen and generally very boxy profile were the complete opposite of the curvy, rounded standard Duple Laser.

Below: Pictured arriving at the East Anglian Transport Museum, Carlton Colville, this was the final Dominant bus body built and was fitted to a Leyland TRCTL11/2RZ. It had a wide, four-leaf, entrance door and seating for 62 in a high-floor saloon. Delaine of Bourne is well-known for running immaculate vehicles and, by the date of the photograph, the vehicle was almost 20 years old. By 1987, when it entered service, this type of high-floor vehicle was becoming obsolete as low-floor buses were increasingly needed to meet access for all regulations. DDA rules changed bus building forever.

The rear offside emergency exit was brought forward half a bay to accommodate the rear engine layout and this door was full-depth to keep access steps inside the body for a cleaner look and safer evacuation if needed. Good luggage space was available between the axles: the advantage of being integrally built without an intrusive chassis. Its front axle had a narrower track than most coaches of its size. The Calypso was finished with the aluminium upright flashes that Duple used on its Laser bodies and the new wider grille/single headlight style.

This collaboration between Bova and Duple only lasted from 1984 until the following year. In the background Bova design engineers were adapting its Futura body for lowheight operation. The coach debuted in 1986 as the Futura FLC (Club), fitted with either a DAF or Cummins engine.

In a further blow for the business, Ford Commercial Vehicles announced in 1985 it was about to pull out of full-size PSV chassis production. Its 10m and 11m models had suffered poor sales at the start of the decade, as longer, air-sprung, powerful coaches won orders over simple, frugal, lightweight offerings. This was a sad loss to both Duple and Plaxton as Ford's only PSV options thereafter would be the Transit or the Cargo lorry chassis for specialist uses.

Another Dennis Javelin, this was a very smart 11m 320-bodied coach that had been delivered new to Bebbs of Llantwit Fardre in Wales. For a period in the early 1990s it operated with Regis Coaches and was being operated by Day's Coaches of Rotherham when recorded here.

The final standard Bedford/Duple product was the 12m air-spring YNV chassis fitted with a 320 body. This coach dated originally to 1986 and, as with Michelotti's design for the Dominant 2, the very deep windscreen was dominated by the driver's instrument binnacle. As a contract/private hire vehicle, the 320 body was a capable and attractive buy.

The Laser and Caribbean both received restyles for the 1985 build season. Bonded glazing was made standard on the Laser 2 as Plaxton had made the same move to revamp its Paramount range in the same year. A new lower front panel moved the grille to a deeper position; the grille was finished in matt black and was of a design with finer horizontal slats. A single square headlight was sited either side and the whole panel was hinged at the bottom, allowing it open forward to access the front lights and radiator, assist with daily checks of coolant and screen-wash. Screen wipers were larger and sat across the bottom of the glass, one above the other.

The Caribbean also gained this drop open front but, when the side trim was altered from polished aluminium to matt black, this made the high-floor/heavyweight luxury coach have a more dull, sterile appearance. The modifications that worked well to make the Laser 2 a valid competitor to the Paramount, in turn ruined its Caribbean stablemate.

These revamps proved ridiculously shortlived and, by the end of 1985, both bodies had been discontinued. Their hasty replacements were two bodies simply titled 320/340 respectively, these numbers related to their height in centimetres; Hestair Duple had clearly ran out of imagination with regard to model names.

Exterior wise, these new ranges were bland, very boxy in appearance and devoid of the shiny bright-work and trim for which Duple had been noted. This aside, the standard height 320 body found many customers as a modern looking 53- to 57-seat contract/private hire coach. The Bedford/Duple connection was still fairly popular with the traditional buyer and the air-sprung, turbo-charged YNV chassis powered a good number of 320 models. The body could be built to 11m length, so the option of the steel-sprung YNT chassis was available also, until GM Bedford decided it had no future in PSV manufacture.

The 320 and 340 carried the windscreen over from the Caribbean and the straight-sided upright looks. New, fussy rear light clusters were recessed in the GRP rear-end, but a very simple front dash panel featured, with no obvious bumpers at either end.

The 320 range was built on the Leyland Tiger, Volvo B10M, GM/Bedford and, with some alterations, the rear-engined DAF SB2300 and Scania K92. Later in 1987, Dennis introduced its Javelin chassis to fill a void left by Bedford and the 320 was built at 11m, 12m and the short 8.5m lengths for Dennis customers.

The taller 340 body, had its windscreen set lower in its body than the Caribbean did, resulting in a downward curve from behind the entrance to meet the front roof edge. Like the previous models, the taller, more expensive of the two possessed the least attractive body. That said, major fleets like National Express and Wallace Arnold bought 340s for their fleets, but not on the scale at which Plaxton was selling its Paramount 3500 range. The 340 only achieved a single batch in the Wallace Arnold fleet, with subsequent orders going to Plaxton and Van Hool. But larger concerns like the Scottish Bus Group and National Express took batches on the Leyland Tiger chassis. Never a stunner on the outside, this model did not encourage many customers to open their cheque books. The 340 was built on DAF, Leyland and Volvo products for those who wanted a functional — if uninspiring — vehicle in their fleet.

Happily, though, it was not all gloomy news for the 1985 season. A new design had had been launched at the 1984 Commercial Motor Show and the first deliveries commenced in the following year. At last, after numerous restyles and revamps of fading models, Duple hit the competition with something stunning — the 425.

This totally new coach was an integral vehicle, built only at 12m length using stainless steel framework in a method known as Cromweld construction. But it was on the outside where the 425 really made an impression. The coach had hints of Neoplan in its appearance. The large windscreen was horizontally divided, the top section raked backwards noticeably above the entrance/driver's cabin. Below a deep area was painted black to give the illusion of even more glass; this disguised the horizontal wiper arms to a degree also. A very upright rear end carried an air ventilation pod above the last side window bay, and on the off-side a door for use on the continent doubled as the emergency exit.

Under its attractive skin, the 425 had two-engine choices — either a DAF 10.6-litre unit or the Cummins L10, fitted at the rear in both cases. It was, at the time, the most aerodynamic coach on the British market, with a drag co-efficiency of 0.425.

The framework beneath this beauty ensured a longevity for the bodywork that Duple was not always renowned for. The 425's high-quality build techniques meant a good number of these were considered worthy of modernising and keeping in operators' fleet strengths. Some 425s received cosmetic tweaks and others were professionally restyled and refurbished; even some almost original 425 models exist at the time of writing — the restyled ones could have long careers ahead still, not something that was achieved by a Laser or Caribbean without serious rebuilding.

Reassuring, if ironic, as the 425 blazed a fresh trail in coach build and design, the single-deck Dominant bus body had remained a constant in the Duple product range since the mid- 1970s, the final vehicle being delivered in 1987.

Originally aimed at the lightweight chassis from Ford and Bedford, the Dominant achieved sales from small/medium independent operators to municipal fleets like Hyndburn and Maidstone, which took batches on the Bedford YRQ, YRT and YMT chassis. The Ford R1014 45-seat bus even broke into National Bus Company subsidiaries South Midland and United Counties and also ventured across the water to join Jersey Motor Transport.

On a smaller scale, the bus body was shortened and reduced in width to fit a batch of Leyland Cubs for Lothian Transport in 1983. A few were built on the Dennis Lancet and Falcon H chassis. The Lancets were 10m buses and some had wheelchair lifts midway; the unusual Falcon H was a rear-engined 11m bus that had two floor level, resulting in a stepped window line.

The Dominant bus sold in smaller numbers on heavyweight chassis from the 1970s as well; operators in hillier parts of the British Isles who wanted more 'grunt' from their vehicles preferred the Leyland Leopard and, to a lesser extent, an AEC

At the time belonging to Grahams, Kelvedon, Essex, this DAF SB2300 was recorded at a busy Great Yarmouth coach park in the mid-1990s. The view shows to good effect the longer front overhang and the shorter wheelbase of this model. Early Scania K92 and K93 models also had set-back front axles that coachbuilders had to accommodate. The Duple 320 body was an attractive body, seating between 55 and 57 passengers. The rearmost row of five seats was raised slightly higher to sit above the rear power unit of the DAF.

Reliance. Leopards were always a popular chassis to operate around Yorkshire, the Pennines and the steep parts of Wales. A few Dominant buses were built on the Volvo B58 in the early 1980s. The final body going on a Leyland Tiger in 1987 for The Delaine of Bourne, Lincolnshire. This still exists in the operator's fleet at the time of writing in smart blue, black and white colours.

The replacement body took a while to materialise and was only built in very small numbers in late 1988 and part of 1989. The style was fairly bland; named the Duple 300 it could be ordered on Dennis, Leyland and Volvo chassis.

Eastern Counties, which by 1989 had been privatised from the NBC, purchased a batch of coach-seated 300-bodied Dennis Javelins for its longer routes. In the same year the operator also bought a number of 11m Javelins with the Derwent 2 bodies from Plaxton, a much more softer, pleasing to the eye body from a personal point of view and as the Scarborough builder won more orders for them — buyers maybe thought like I did.

Some 300s were built on the 11m Leyland Tiger and Scottish operator Hutchinson of Overtown took a few on the Volvo B10M coach chassis. This operator had for years been a fan of the AEC Reliance/Dominant bus combination to cover its service duties. The single-deck market was on the verge of a massive change and high-floor vehicles on this work were becoming unwelcome.

A shift to low-floor, buggy and wheelchair-friendly buses was sweeping the industry, as the flood of Transit-style mini-buses had done on deregulation of services in 1986 when Leyland Sherpas, Mercedes 608s and Ford Transits were flying all over the place and being bought in huge numbers.

Rear-engined, lightweight, low-floor was the place to be in the single-deck market from 1989 onwards and Duple wasted no time in producing a pleasant,

The high-floor Duple 340 was the successor to the Caribbean body, but sales were poor in comparison to the main competitors in the sector. By this date, the late 1980s, foreign imports, from manufacturers such as Van Hool and Jonckheere, had become increasingly popular as a result of their build quality and attention to detail.

simple body for the new Dennis Dart underframe. Built in three lengths, it featured deep, low-level windows, a curved, barrel-style screen and a very shallow roof profile. Duple sold decent numbers, albeit in small batches.

Council-owned Great Yarmouth Transport bought a pair of Dartlines but, like other operators, experienced problems with the sun obscuring the destination display. The display was first placed above the driver and behind the curved windscreen, but reflective sunlight played havoc for passengers standing at bus stops and the vehicles went back to Blackpool to have a cumbersome, oblong display placed above the screen. Not gelling with the shallow roof, visually this ruined the low-profile concept of the bodywork. Carlyle bought the design rights for this body when Duple collapsed.

This was the pinnacle of Duple design and build. The 425 was the most aerodynamic coach body on the market. It was steel framed using the Cromweld method of construction. The registration was originally carried by a South Wales Transport AEC Regent V and was transferred to the coach when the latter was acquired by the operator (fleet number 131). The registration was subsequently transferred to another SWT coach — a Duple 320 rebodied Leyland Leopard No 194 that had previously been registered AFH 192T.

The Last Years

A management buyout of Duple took it from the Hestair Group to the newly formed Trinity Holdings during 1988. The idea was for it to be run by people on the inside at Blackpool and hopefully steer the business into the 1990s in good shape.

Biggest rival Plaxton had acquired some large fleet customers that Duple was not attracting and, therefore, having 'coach men' at the helm should have helped to redress the balance.

National Express had standardised on a vehicle called the Expressliner, a high-floor Plaxton Paramount III with very little exterior trim on the trusty, fast Volvo B10M chassis. This represented a missed opportunity for a coachbuilder desperately needing work as the 340 body spectacularly failed to compete in the Paramount's market.

The Dartline's fortunes dived after a reputation for needing rectifying soon after purchase, losing orders to the Reeve Burgess Pointer body, the Alexander Dash and Wright Handybus. This market grew massively for these builders — another missed opportunity for Duple.

In fact, the only body to keep its credibility in the range was the 320 coach, latterly enjoying good sales on the Dennis Javelin chassis at 8.5m, 11m and maximum 12m lengths — filling a void that Bedford had left open. This body had been well liked since its appearance in late 1985 on the Leyland Tiger or Bedford YNT/YNV.

But no coachbuilder could survive as a large employer only making one popular body. Trinity Holdings took the harsh decision to end 70 years of Duple production during 1989. The Dartline design and manufacturing rights were sold to Carlyle Ltd, whilst the coach designs and production rights were purchased by Plaxton. During 1990, 25 12m 320 bodies were built at the latter's Scarborough factory, all on the Leyland Tiger chassis — itself also nearing the end of production. These differed very little from Duple days but were badged as the Plaxton 321. Twelve 425 models were produced at the Carrossie Lorraine factory in France, which was also owned by Plaxton by then.

After 70 years of building — some models terrific, some terrible — Duple will be forever remembered by operators who built their businesses with Vistas, Vegas and Viceroys, swung through the 1960s with SBs, six-wheelers and seaside trips, struggled through the 1970s with its strikes, short working weeks and sunburn, and entered the 1980s as unemployment increased and the chassis that Duple needed deceased. Duple began the decade a Dominant force and ended the decade a exhausted corpse!

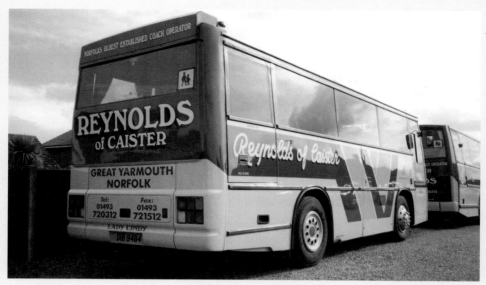

Above: Duple shortened its standard-height 320 body for fitting on the smallest 8.5m Dennis Javelin chassis. This well cared for example was originally new with Mackie of Alloa in Scotland in 1989. It passed to the ownership of Reynolds of Caister in 2008 from Vallances of Nottingham. The name 'Lady Cindy' comes from that of the writer's wife.

Top right: This Dennis Javelin/Duple 300 is recorded with Eastern Counties in service at Castle Meadow, in Norwich. The 11m vehicle had been delivered new to the operator as the last of a batch of five dual-purpose 48-seat vehicles in November and December 1989.

Bottom right: Duple developed the Dartline body for Dennis's Dart midibus chassis, a rear-engined low-floor single-deck model that was ironically to become very popular in the years following Duple's demise in 1989. Following the end of Duple, the design was sold to Carlyle, which manufactured the body during 1990. G515 VYE was one of a batch of 27 delivered to London Buses in March and April 1990 but is seen here in the livery of Weaverbus for use on a service from Weymouth to Lulworth Cove. Weaverbus ceased to operate the route in 2005 and the bus was sold to a collector in Surrey.

Index